A Global Dialogue on Federalism
Booklet Series
Volume II

DIALOGUES ON DISTRIBUTION OF POWERS AND RESPONSIBILITIES IN FEDERAL COUNTRIES

EDITED BY RAOUL BLINDENBACHER
AND ABIGAIL OSTIEN

Published for

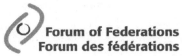
Forum of Federations
Forum des fédérations

and

iacfs
INTERNATIONAL ASSOCIATION OF
CENTERS FOR FEDERAL STUDIES

by

McGill-Queen's University Press
Montreal & Kingston · London · Ithaca

© McGill-Queen's University Press 2005
ISBN 0-7735-2940-3

Legal deposit second quarter 2005
Bibliothèque nationale du Québec

Printed in Canada on acid-free paper that is 100% ancient forest free
(100% post-consumer recycled), processed chlorine free.

McGill-Queen's University Press acknowledges the support of the Canada
Council for the Arts for our publishing program. We also acknowledge
the financial support of the Government of Canada through the Book
Publishing Industry Development Program (BPIDP) for our publishing
activities.

Library and Archives Canada Cataloguing in Publication

Dialogues on distribution of powers and responsibilities in federal countries /
edited by Raoul Blindenbacher and Abigail Ostien.

(A global dialogue on federalism booklet series; v. 2)
ISBN 0-7735-2940-3

  1. Federal government. I. Blindenbacher, Raoul II. Ostien, Abigail J.,
1971– III. Forum of Federations IV. International Association of Centers
for Federal Studies V. Series: Global dialogue on federalism
booklet series; v. 2.

JC355.D523 2005   321'.02   C2005-900714-1

This book was typeset by Interscript Inc. in 10/12 Baskerville.

Contents

Preface   vii

DIALOGUE INSIGHTS

Australia: A Quiet Revolution in the Balance of Power   3
CLEMENT MACINTYRE/JOHN WILLIAMS

Belgium: Continuing Changes in a New Federal Structure   6
HUGUES DUMONT/SÉBASTIEN VAN DROOGHENBROECK/
NICOLAS LAGASSE/MARC VAN DER HULST

Brazil: Federation Building and Social Welfare   9
MARCELO PIANCASTELLI DE SIQUEIRA

Canada: Competition within Cooperative Federalism   12
RICHARD SIMEON

Germany: Länder Implementing Federal Legislation   15
HANS-PETER SCHNEIDER

India: Continuity and Change in the Federal Union   18
GEORGE MATHEW

Mexico: A Historic Election Brings Pressures
for Decentralization   21
MANUEL GONZÁLEZ OROPEZA

Nigeria: Over-Centralization after Decades of Military Rule   24
J. ISAWA ELAIGWU

Spain: A Unique Model of State Autonomy   27
XAVIER BERNADÍ GIL/CLARA VELASCO

Switzerland: Seeking a Balance between Shared Rule
and Self-Rule 30
SARAH BYRNE/THOMAS FLEINER

The United States of America: A Federal Government of
Limited Powers 33
ELLIS KATZ

Comparative Reflections 36
RONALD L. WATTS

Glossary 39

Contributors 47

Participating Experts 49

Preface

After having published our first booklet on federal constitutions, we are pleased to introduce the second booklet in the Global Dialogue on Federalism series. This booklet explores the distribution and functioning of powers in federal systems. It reflects several lively dialogues that occurred at roundtables in Australia, Belgium, Brazil, Canada, Germany, India, Mexico, Nigeria, Spain, Switzerland, and the United States. Those who participated in the dialogue events – both practitioners and academics – are experts in their respective countries, all contributing a diversity of viewpoints.

The content of these short articles provides the reader with a brief synopsis of how powers and responsibilities are distributed in each featured country and the current challenges to each system. The authors' words are a reflection of their own understanding of the issues and of the insights gained during the dialogue events.

Among the questions explored in the articles are: What are the roots of the federation and how does this account for the present system? What are the "nuts and bolts" of the system of distribution in the country? Has the system become more centralized or less and is it currently striving for either? What are the main reasons the system has evolved and through what means (e.g., constitutional amendment, judicial interpretations, political maneuvering)? What body, if any, has been set up to resolve conflicts between entities? What are the main problems the system currently faces?

The exploration of these questions forms the body of the booklet in country articles entitled "Dialogue Insights." The concluding chapter by Ronald L. Watts summarizes commonalities and differences in the featured countries. A glossary at the end of the booklet contributes to the accessible and educative nature of this publication, laying the groundwork for a more comprehensive book on this same theme. As such, it is our intention that the articles presented here will serve to provide an entry point for Volume II of the book series, *Distribution of Powers and Responsibilities in Federal Countries*, wherein the same authors explore the topic in much more detail.

The booklet is one outcome of a much greater project: *A Global Dialogue on Federalism*, a joint program of the Forum of Federations and the International Association of Centers for Federal Studies (IACFS). It is an exploration of federal governance by theme, which aims to bring experts together to inspire new ideas and fill a gap in comparative information on federal governance. The first theme examined the origins, structure, and change of 12 federal constitutions; examples of future themes include legislative and executive governance, fiscal federalism, and foreign relations.

Each theme exploration entails a multiple-staged process. First, a "theme coordinator" is chosen, who makes use of the most current research on the theme to create an internationally comprehensive set of questions covering institutional provisions and how they work in practice. This set of questions, or "theme template," is the foundation of the program, as it guides the dialogue at the roundtables and forms the outline for the theme book. The theme coordinator also selects a representative sample of federal countries and recommends a coordinator – the authors of these articles – for each featured country.

Next, each country coordinator invites a select and diverse group of practicing and academic experts to participate in a roundtable in his or her country, guided by the theme template. The goal is to create the most accurate picture of the theme in each country by inviting experts with diverse viewpoints and experience who are prepared to share with and learn from others in a non-politicized environment.

At the end of the day, the coordinators are equipped to write an article that reflects the highlights of the dialogue from each country roundtable. The articles presented here have been generated from such an exchange.

Once each country has held its roundtable, representatives gather at an international roundtable. The representatives are experts who share their varied experiences and perspectives, as well as the knowledge gained from their country's roundtable, to identify commonalities and differences and to generate new insights.

As indicated above, country coordinators also write a detailed chapter for the theme book. The chapters reflect the fact that their authors were able to explore the theme from a global vantage point, resulting in a truly comparative exploration of the topic.

In keeping with its more limited scope and the intent to share the insights gained within a short time frame, the booklet is published soon after the international roundtable. It is widely distributed to a broad audience and is available in several languages. The book series provides far more detailed information about each country as well as a chapter summarizing comparative conclusions. The program also includes a website that provides on-line access to a discussion forum, which enables people around the world to become involved in the Global Dialogue. The discussion forum as well as all Global Dialogue articles and chapters are available on-line at the same address at www.forumfed.org.

The Global Dialogue on Federalism Series continues a tradition of Forum of Federations' publications either independently, or in partnership with other organizations. The Forum has produced a variety of books and multimedia material. Refer to the Forum's website listed above for more information on the Forum's publications and activities. The website also contains links to other organizations and an online library.

Finally, we would like to express our appreciation to the authors of the second theme booklet for their contributions to this volume. Special thanks are due to Ronald L. Watts for writing the final chapter, "Comparative Reflections" and for offering his feedback on the booklet as a whole. We wish to acknowledge the experts who took part in the dialogue events for providing a diversity of perspectives that helped to shape the articles themselves. Their names are listed at the end of the booklet. John Kincaid, Cheryl Saunders, and the rest of the Global Dialogue Editorial Board have offered their invaluable advice and expertise. Thank you to Alan Fenna and Thomas Hueglin for doing the pain-staking work of creating the glossary. We would like to acknowledge the support offered by several staff members at the Forum of Federations. They include: Barbara Brook, Global Dialogue Program Manager, as well as Rhonda Dumas, Mahalya Havard, Karl Nerenberg, and Carl Stieren. Finally, we thank the staff at McGill-Queen's University Press for offering their support and advice throughout the publication process.

Readers of this booklet are encouraged to use the knowledge gained to inspire new solutions, thereby strengthening democratic governance, and to join the many Global Dialogue participants around the world to expand and strengthen the growing international network on federalism.

Raoul Blindenbacher and Abigail Ostien, editors

DIALOGUES ON DISTRIBUTION OF POWERS
AND RESPONSIBILITIES IN FEDERAL COUNTRIES

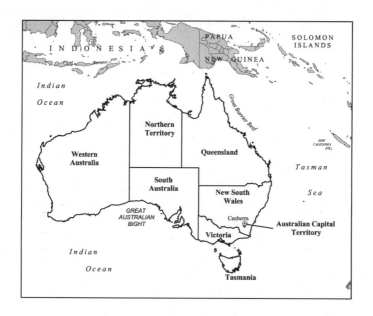

Australia:
A Quiet Revolution in the Balance
of Power

CLEMENT MACINTYRE
AND JOHN WILLIAMS

Despite very few formal constitutional changes over the past century, significant revisions effectively have been made to the distribution of powers and responsibilities in the Australian federation. The national sphere of government, or Commonwealth, has gradually acquired more powers at the expense of the states in order to meet the changing role and responsibilities of government. Australia's federal system thus has evolved, not so much through deliberate amendment, but as a result of judicial interpretation of the Constitution and deft political manoeuvring.

Australia is simultaneously one of the youngest democracies and one of the oldest federations. In 1901, the six Australian colonies united in "one indissoluble Federal Commonwealth under the Crown of the United Kingdom." That decision was the result of deliberation, compromise, and debate over the needs and aspirations of the community –

though notably it excluded any consultation with the indigenous people. In the century since federation, there has been a quiet revolution in the balance of powers and responsibilities between the centre and the states. Today, Australia is one of the more centralized federal systems in the world.

The drafting of the Australian Constitution was a project in comparative constitutional law and politics. The framers, brought up on a diet of responsible government modelled on the Westminster system, had to find a means to accommodate the benefits of union and the need of the colonies for autonomy. To the system of responsible government they grafted a federal structure. Inspiration for Australian federalism can most obviously be found in the United States. Many of the framers had visited the U.S. and had studied American constitutional law. Ironically, the framers chose the American model of federation over the Canadian system, because they were concerned about the latter's perceived centralizing federalism. History would show their perceptions to be incorrect.

The framers opted for a concurrent system of powers and responsibilities, following the example of the United States Constitution. They provided in their Constitution a list of areas over which the Commonwealth could make concurrent laws with the states, including taxation, the regulation of certain types of corporations, immigration and marriage, and divorce. In granting to the Commonwealth Parliament a defined list of powers, the framers left the residue to the states, as a matter of law. Thus areas such as criminal law, the control of land and health care remain with the states under the Constitution and ensure a continuing and significant role for them. The powers that are expressly allocated to the Commonwealth consist of the minimum deemed necessary to create a nation in Australia in 1901.

The Constitution allows for the Commonwealth to have exclusive powers over defence, duties of customs and excise, currency, and what are considered "Commonwealth places," such as the seat of government in Canberra. Further, when laws of the Commonwealth and the states deal with the same subject matter, such as the regulation of corporations, the Commonwealth law will prevail to the extent of any inconsistencies.

This basic scheme, established in 1901, has been resistant to formal change. Constitutional change requires endorsement by the people at referendum. Over the century there have been 44 referendums proposed, only eight of which have been successful, notably the granting of Commonwealth legislative power over indigenous Australians in 1967. Most recently, Australians rejected the attempt to sever ties with the British monarchy and establish Australia as a republic. The cause of this resistance has exercised the minds of political scientists and would-be reformers. Ultimately, it appears that constitutional reform is dependent on two factors: bipartisan political support and no perceived increase in the power of the Commonwealth. However, even these elements have not always assured success.

Despite the small number of formal amendments made to it, the Australian federal system has been transformed significantly, largely due to interpretations of the Constitution by the High Court. The Court, established in 1903, is a court of appeal from the Supreme Court of each state and other federal courts and is the interpreter of the Constitution. Its role as final arbiter of Australian law was initially overshadowed by the opportunity for appeals to the British Privy Council. The option to appeal to Britain was ended in a series of legislative actions starting in the 1960s and ending in 1986.

The High Court has been a prime innovator in Australian federalism. The first few decades of Australian federalism witnessed an attempt by the Court to maintain the federal balance that existed at the union of the colonies. Soon, though, the Court dramatically changed tack and in 1920 permitted the Commonwealth to exercise its legislative powers without the implied restriction of the previous decades. This, together with changes in the political landscape after the Second World War, allowed the Commonwealth to emerge as the significant actor within Australian federalism.

As a result of constitutional interpretation and deft political manoeuvring, the Commonwealth has come to dominate the Australian federation. Control of direct and indirect taxation has allowed it to use its financial muscle to force the compliance of the states, even when it lacks direct legislative capacity. Today, education, health, and law and order are dominated, in varying degrees, by the Commonwealth's policy agenda. Moreover, Commonwealth power in relation to the making and implementation of international treaties effectively has extended its power further, as the numbers and range of such treaties have increased. This has proved controversial in many areas such as environmental protection, human rights, and industrial relations.

Since its inception, Australian federalism has consistently attempted to draw clear legal lines of power and responsibilities between the Commonwealth and the states. Even though the lines have gradually shifted, through a combination of cooperation, litigation, and history, the Australian federation has proved a relatively successful system of governance.

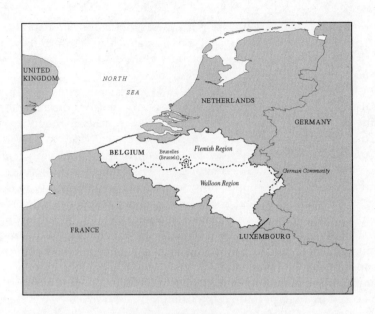

Belgium:
Continuing Changes
in a New Federal Structure

HUGUES DUMONT, SÉBASTIEN VAN
DROOGHENBROECK, NICOLAS LAGASSE,
AND MARC VAN DER HULST

The transformation of Belgium from a unitary to a federal state is quite a recent phenomenon from a legal point of view. It began in 1970 and has continued in successive waves in 1980, 1988–89, 1993, and 2001. Despite the recent changes, there continues to be political pressure for greater devolution of power away from the national government. At present, no one would hazard a guess where this movement will end and what form the result will take.

The changes in Belgium since 1970 have certain similarities to the evolution of the European Union, but in reverse. Both were pragmatic movements undertaken in small steps with no clearly defined goal at the outset, with the main difference being that the EU has become more centralized, while Belgium has become more decentralized.

Belgian federalism has four primary traits: *dissociation, superposition, asymmetry,* and a *dual nature.* These characteristics were important in 1970, and still are so today.

1. *Dissociation.* Unlike most major federations, Belgian federalism does not stem from the association of formerly sovereign political entities, but from the devolution from a formerly unitary state. The centrifugal character of this development explains certain aspects of the distribution of powers between the federal state and the various "federated entities." The federated entities have only those powers that are expressly assigned to them; residual powers belong to the federal state. It was originally foreseen that this distribution of powers would be reversed. However, such an inversion would require the powers remaining with the federal order to be formally identified, restricting the Belgian government's future capacity to act in new areas of jurisdiction. This reversal of residual powers was considered too risky for the current political agenda. The distribution of powers is based on jurisdictional exclusivity – that is, for each issue one sole authority (either the federal order or the constituent units) is assigned to "legislate, execute, and finance" – and generally precludes overlapping jurisdictions. There do remain exceptions and compromises to this rule, however.

2. *Superposition.* Belgium distinguishes itself from classical federal models by having two distinct types of federated political entities: the language communities and the territorial regions. The three communities are the Flemish-speaking, French-speaking, and German-speaking communities. The "community phenomenon" was the result of Flemish demands, and has its roots in the minority status in which the Flemish language and culture was placed in the 19th and early 20th centuries. Community responsibilities include cultural matters, "personal" matters – that is, matters dealing with relations between individuals, such as youth protection – and, with some exceptions, education and the use of language.

There are also three regions: the Flemish, Walloon, and Brussels-Capital regions. The "regional phenomenon" was introduced in answer to pressure from the Walloons in the south of the country. Politicians from the south responded to the aging and decline of the Walloon economy in the 1960s by seeking further economic control and autonomy. Through successive reforms, regions have received such powers as land management in a broad sense (e.g., environment, land use), economic policy (e.g., employment, foreign trade, agriculture), and the organization and control of decentralized political entities (e.g., provinces and municipalities).

Each community and region has a legislature, called the council, and an executive, termed the government. As a result, the number of lawmakers in Belgian federalism has increased substantially, and consequently, so have the opportunities for conflict between their powers. In order to resolve such conflicts, a constitutional court (*Cour d'arbitrage/Arbitragehof*) was created in 1980. In addition, the federated entities and the federal state can draw up co-operation agreements with one another to overcome disagreements. If necessary, special institutional reform laws can actually require that such co-operation agreements be drawn up.

3. *Asymmetry*. Belgian federalism is also characterized by asymmetry, which produces and permits differences in the organization and powers of the federated political entities. As an example, the status of the Brussels-Capital region is not the same as that of the other two regions; in certain matters, it remains under the control of the federal state. Another example is that, under Article 137 of the Constitution, the councils of the French-speaking and Flemish-speaking communities may take on the powers of the Walloon and Flemish regions, respectively. Such a "fusion" has been carried out in Flanders, but not in the south.

The Constitution also permits the French-speaking community to transfer the exercise of some of its powers to the Walloon Region, in the unilingual French-speaking part of the country, and to the "French-language Community Commission" (*Commission communautaire française*) in Brussels. Some of these transfers have already been carried out, meaning that community powers are no longer identical in the north and south of the country.

4. *Dual Nature*. Finally, Belgian federalism has a dual nature *(la bipolarité)*. The legal evolution of any federation is determined by the social forces present in the country. As another demonstration of its difference from other federations, the force in Belgium has a distinctly dual nature, with the two partners being the Flemish and Francophone communities.

> These forces and the tensions they generate are the true engines of Belgian institutional evolution.

These forces and the tensions they generate are the true engines of Belgian institutional evolution. As a result, the successive institutional reforms have developed as pragmatic and consensual solutions to crises, rather than as a sequence of deliberate steps toward a clear and pre-established objective. The complexity of Belgian institutions is the consequence of this pragmatism. But this complexity is also the price that has had to be paid, to avoid more extreme conflicts between the communities.

Brazil:
Federation Building
and Social Welfare

MARCELO PIANCASTELLI DE SIQUEIRA

Brazil has a vast territory and a complex and financially asymmetric federal system. The country has been trying to achieve economic stability, while struggling against entrenched social inequalities and regional disparities. The objectives of the present constitution are the consolidation of democracy, decentralization of government, and improvement of the social conditions of the population. Constitutional rules have been changing over time, largely to adapt to the changing economic context. However, Brazil's republican federalism as a form of government organization has shown remarkable stability.

Attempts to implement a federal form of government can be traced back to 1831. However, it was the organization constitutionally into states in 1891 that led to the first republican federal constitution. The present constitution was adopted in 1988. It demonstrates a clear motivation for decentralization in order to bring power closer to the people, and has been in constant evolution through intra-constitutional legislation, the so-called "Complementary Laws."

The drafters of the current federal constitution aimed to achieve a decentralized organization of government in order to enhance the democratic process in the country. Article 1 introduces the basis of federalism as a permanent link between the federal government, states, and municipalities. The aim was to promote sovereignty, citizenship, the dignity of human beings, the social value of labour, the contribution of private business, and political plurality. Article 2 states that the fundamental objective of the federal republic is to build a free, just and united society, to guarantee national development, to eradicate poverty and to reduce social and regional inequalities.

> The drafters of the current federal constitution aimed to achieve a decentralized organization of government in order to enhance the democratic process in the country.

However, history shows that the shape of Brazilian federalism has neither been one of centralization nor decentralization. It has consistently been adjusted according to the political and economic context of the times. Since the first attempt to implement a federal system in 1831, Brazil's constitutional development has not been systematic. Under the terms of the 1988 Constitution, Brazilian federalism can be best described as "cooperative" or "collusive," depending upon the issue under discussion, although decentralization has recently been a constant imperative. Political circumstances have also played a key role in determining the direction of Brazil's constitutional history.

Observers believe that federalism in Brazil must advance in the following directions: improved management of the metropolitan areas, improvement of public services (water supply, sanitation, health, education, social assistance), assistance for infants and the elderly, development of organizations for local consultation and, most importantly, budgetary laws must become mandatory.

The budgetary system is one of the major challenges facing the Brazilian federation. There are currently three separate budgets, one for each order of government, which are not well coordinated and do not share the same priorities. Decentralization within the 1988 Constitution renders the coordination of macroeconomic policies more difficult and it is now virtually impossible to identify where public money has been spent. Budgets in Brazil are not mandatory, but only permissive, except for those earmarked as public expenditures. In this sense, they are only indicative of the assignments to which public expenditures may be allocated.

There are also other reasons why Brazilian federalism faces considerable challenges in the future. One of which is the way the 1988 Constitution was designed. It aimed to introduce new democratic rules and to address current social and regional inequalities. It embodied an on-going tendency towards decentralization. This tendency resulted in a number of public services, especially in the social sectors, being decentralized. Unfortunately, this has taken place without the appropriate budget accountability and with an unclear distribution of powers and responsibilities.

The substantial increase in transfers to the states has had a great impact on the public finances of the country. The social nature of these objectives was never in dispute, but the exact source of funds to finance them was. Fifteen years after the adoption of the Constitution, public finances have not yet reached a fiscal equilibrium. The national government is still struggling to raise revenues and reorganize public expenditure in order to achieve permanent and sustainable rates of growth. The states and municipalities, for their part, have constitutional and statutory authority to raise revenues. However, they have only recently engaged in a disciplined fiscal policy, since a Fiscal Responsibility Law was approved in mid-2000.

The excessive emphasis on decentralization has thus become a source of great difficulty. In the present Brazilian context, it can be regarded as an effective mechanism for the supply and quality of public goods and services, as well as a means to achieve greater transparency. However, it can be costly. Some states are much better positioned to absorb these costs than others, exacerbating the regional inequalities that the Constitution is designed to address.

Stable fiscal equilibrium is another important issue for the Brazilian federation, especially in terms of greater economic stability and reduction of regional and social inequalities. The structure of Brazil's constitutional revenue sharing system is unbalanced. Because the constitutional transfer of funds is asymmetrical and not yet clearly aimed to deal with social priorities and equal opportunities, Brazilian federalism is failing in its attempts to address the regional and income disparities in the country.

Canada:
Competition within
Cooperative Federalism

RICHARD SIMEON

You will only get a partial picture of "who does what" if you read the Canadian Constitution Act of 1867. The text of sections 91 and 92 of the Act defines the division of powers and responsibilities in Canada, but gives only a partial picture of the real balance of powers. The division of powers is constantly in flux. The weight of influence has swung from federal dominance, to classical dualist federalism, to a reassertion of federal influence, to the present, in which two powerful orders of government use many jurisdictional, bureaucratic, financial and political levers to shape policy over broad areas. As new policy concerns such as the environment have arisen, both have the will and means to become involved. "Watertight compartments" have been supplanted

> "Watertight compartments" have been supplanted by overlapping, sharing, and interdependence.

by overlapping, sharing, and interdependence. Central to the Canadian policy-making process is a complex mixture of cooperation and competition among governments.

Amendment remains rare and difficult, but judicial decisions, intergovernmental agreements, and financial transfers have allowed the Constitution to adapt to new needs. Major changes were made in 1982, when a Charter of Rights was adopted and authority for amending the Constitution was "patriated" from Great Britain, so Canada no longer had to ask the UK parliament at Westminster for official constitutional amendments. Two subsequent attempts to bring in significant amendments both failed.

Many factors explain the changing patterns of Canadian federalism. First is demographic change. The Canada of 1867 with four provinces and just 3.5 million people is now a country of 32 million, ten provinces, and three territories, touching on three oceans. A once largely rural country is now one of the world's most urbanized. A society originally made up almost entirely of people of French and British descent (together with the largely displaced Aboriginal inhabitants) is now among the world's most diverse and multicultural. A second major factor is the importance of international agreements and trade. Canada is economically integrated into the North American market. This change has had enormous impacts on policy agendas and citizen expectations. A third set of factors has involved regional differences over concepts of citizenship, identity, and society. The fundamental division is language. French-speaking Canadians, concentrated in Quebec, have a strong sense of national identity and a distinct approach to the role of the state. Quebec has resisted increased federal power and today it is a powerful advocate for "asymmetry." Other provinces also have strong identities, distinctive policy concerns, and strong provincial governments. A single country-wide policy is often inappropriate and unworkable.

The interaction of these forces, which often pull in different directions, makes it difficult to characterize the division of powers in simple terms. Ottawa is largely responsible for international affairs, security, macroeconomic policy, immigration and citizenship. However, provinces also have an important voice in these areas. They are largely responsible for education, health care, welfare, economic development, and regulation of industry. However, Ottawa is also involved in these areas through transfers to provincial governments, and through its program for equalization, designed to ensure that poorer provinces are able to meet their responsibilities without undue levels of taxation. This has led to "collaborative federalism" with several intergovernmental accords respecting economic and social issues, health care and the environment.

But who does what is never a fully settled issue, and a number of important questions confront citizens and governments today.

First among these is the concern about fiscal imbalance. Provinces assert that there is a mismatch between their responsibilities and the revenues available to them. The federal government stresses its own fiscal needs and the provincial ability to raise taxes.

Another debate involves "national standards" as opposed to provincial variation. National citizenship implies that common standards should apply to all Canadians, while federalism is predicated on policy variation. How to find the balance in areas such as health care?

A relatively new issue is participation in the global and North American economies. Are provinces and local governments best placed to adapt to global imperatives, or is a stronger federal hand necessary to ensure that Canada speaks with one voice abroad?

The Constitution assigns the same responsibilities to all provinces, but would "asymmetry" better reflect the reality of the country? In law and practice, considerable divergence among provinces has developed. Would increased asymmetry strengthen or weaken the federation?

Canada wavers between competitive and collaborative federalism. Some argue that effective policy requires joint decision making, given the extensive overlap in responsibilities. Others suggest that governments should compete in an adversarial process, to ensure policy innovation and responsiveness.

External shocks – oil prices, natural catastrophes, and health emergencies, such as the outbreak of SARS – have recently hit Canada and many other countries. Divided responsibility and intergovernmental rivalries have undermined effective policy responses to them. Canadian governments need to improve their capacity to respond to future shocks.

Local governments are under provincial jurisdiction with no independent constitutional status. Yet, they provide a wide range of services to Canadians. There have been recent moves to enhance the autonomy and financial base of municipalities, and to give them a place in Canadian multilevel governance.

Aboriginal peoples have asserted their right to constitute a "third order" of government in Canada. Their claims to land rights and self-government have received strong support from the courts. It is critical for Canada to design models of self-governments, to meet the needs of Aboriginal citizens, most of who now live in urban areas.

The division of powers in Canada today remains a work in progress, its future to be determined as in the past by pragmatic accommodation, within the context of the Constitution and the broad contextual factors noted above. As Canadians work through these issues, they will both learn from and contribute to the experience of others.

Germany:
Länder Implementing
Federal Legislation

HANS-PETER SCHNEIDER

Germany's federal system is characterized by the principle of "strict separation" of responsibilities between the federation and the *Länder* (i.e., the constituent states). Each order is accountable for its own decisions, even when a federal law delegates power to *Land* parliaments. To enforce this principle, the Federal Constitutional Court (FCC) has prohibited mixed administration and mixed financing. However, the German federation is not based on two completely distinct and separate columns of federal and *Land* powers with no connections. Instead there is a concentration of legislative functions in the federal government and of administrative powers in the *Länder*. The *Länder* actually implement a large part of federal legislation, as well as their own laws.

Germany's constitution, the Basic Law, makes a distinction between three types of federal powers: exclusive, concurrent, and framework jurisdictions. The exclusive powers of the Federation read very much like the list of congressional powers in the United States Constitution: foreign affairs, defence, citizenship, movement of goods and persons, communications, and federal taxes. The list of concurrent legislative powers is very extensive. It includes most of the authority over economic and social matters, including welfare, social insurance, labour law, economic regulation, agriculture, and the protection of environment. Finally, there are framework laws, which lay down basic principles and leave their elaboration to the *Länder*. The list of possible subjects of framework legislation is relatively brief, but it also includes much of what are attributed to the *Länder* expressly: higher education, the press and film industry, land reform, and regional planning. The fundamental requirement of framework legislation, the Federal Constitutional Court has specified, is that it leave significant leeway to the *Länder* implementing its provisions.

One of the most surprising aspects of the German administrative system is that most federal laws are carried out by the *Länder*. The basic principle is that the *Länder* shall implement federal legislation as matters of their own concern, as long as the Basic Law does not provide otherwise. The opposite is strictly forbidden; the federation is not allowed to carry out any state law. Therefore, direct federal executive powers are very limited and provided for only in areas in which unified administration is considered to be essential.

However the federal government still has the means to influence the *Länder* in their execution of federal laws. It may regulate *Land* agencies that administer federal laws. It may also confine *Land* administrative discretion by issuing administrative guidelines, and may issue by-laws that bind third parties as well. There may be federal supervision to ensure that the *Länder* carry out federal laws, and federal observers can be dispatched to state agencies for this purpose. Finally, there can be an intermediate form of administration in which the *Länder* enforce federal laws as "agents" of the federation, subject to binding federal instructions.

In fact, the political scope for a *Land* to take action has been considerably reduced in the past fifty years, and the high degree of intertwining of policy-making has reduced the transparency and public control of the decision-making process. These developments in recent decades have actually led to a concentration of powers at both governmental levels, at the level of the federal government on the one hand, and among the entirety of the *Länder* on the other hand, with power and also finances approximately equally distributed. However, these power blocks – having a deleterious effect on political accountability – are so closely linked with each other that hardly anything can be moved politically. The federal government and the *Länder* agree on the diagnosis of immobility, but do not agree on the proper therapy for it.

> The federal government and the *Länder* agree on the diagnosis of immobility, but do not agree on the proper therapy for it.

This immobility can be traced to the 1980s and 1990s when the political decision-making process in Germany became increasingly cumbersome. In fact there was a growing social awareness of the need for fundamental reforms. This awareness met, however, with little response in political practice. The legislative process was blocked as a result of different majorities in the *Bundestag* and the *Bundesrat*, the lower and upper houses of the legislature. The legislative authority of the federal government has grown continually while, correspondingly, the *Länder* have less and less legislative authority and are now virtually only responsible for the administration and the implementation of legislation. In the meantime the framework conditions for this distribution of responsibilities have certainly been fundamentally altered by German unification and by the progress of the European integration process. Thus, in the long term the current arrangement threatens to weaken the political capacity for action.

The processes of European integration and economic globalization have also fundamentally altered the basic conditions for political management in federal countries. These processes point to the need to strengthen the legislative authority of the *Land* level of government. The integration of international markets demands ever-greater specialisation from businesses in countries with high production costs. As a consequence, sectoral and regional differentiation is becoming increasingly important in the competition between locations. In countries like Germany this is leading to a growing importance of the *Länder* as economic policy actors. These changing fundamental conditions for German federalism are already sufficient to make clear that a review of the German constitution has become a pressing political issue. At the core of the issue lies the question of the distribution and disentangling of federal and *Länder* responsibilities, as well as a reform of the financial constitution.

The "fossilised" federal structures of the constitution hardly allow for flexible reactions to modern societal changes. While market forces and their systems of distribution demand a more flexible capacity for reaction from the political system, the constitutional reality in Germany, as a result of joint tasks and joint taxes, the integrated system of tax revenue redistribution ("equalization scheme"), and the continual extension of legislation requiring *Bundesrat* consent, have left the political system even less flexible.

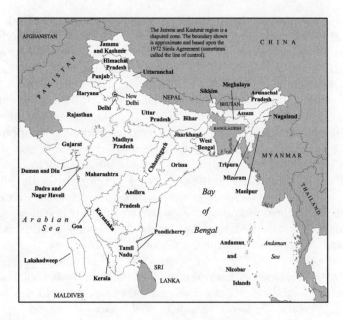

The Jammu and Kashmir region is a disputed zone. The boundary shown is approximate and based upon the 1972 Simla Agreement (sometimes called the line of control).

India:
Continuity and Change
in the Federal Union

GEORGE MATHEW

For more than a decade, India has been experiencing pressures for decentralization, with the states demanding greater say in, and control over economic development. Subnational units in India are expected to contribute to the strength of the country as a whole, but recently the states have been protesting any political interference from the central government in New Delhi. The states have also taken exception to the accumulation of taxation powers by the national government, which has left them financially weakened. These new political pressures are a reversal of the previous trend, which has seen a gradual centralization of powers and responsibilities.

India's complex federal structure was established in the immediate aftermath of Independence in 1949–50. India is a Union of states which consists of 28 full-fledged states, six Union Territories (governed directly by the federal government), one National Capital Territory, and more than a dozen self-governing sub-state units like autonomous regional and district councils. All these structures of governance, along with local governments, draw their authority from the Constitution of India (except Jammu and Kashmir, which has its own constitution). The Constitution distributes powers both symmetrically – for example, the 7th schedule makes distribution of powers symmetric between federal and state governments – and asymmetrically, through several articles like those dealing exclusively with tribal communities, ethnic minorities, and protective development of select regional and sub-regional people. This structure of power distribution and power-sharing arrangements produces a highly complex form of federalism.

> These new political pressures are a reversal of the previous trend, which has seen a gradual centralization of powers and responsibilities.

Within India, there are both centralizing and decentralizing political pressures. On one hand are the imperatives of maintaining national unity and integrity. On the other are the varying requirements of economic development across regions, class, caste, and other geographical and ethnological differences. Although the federal Union consists of a complex network of authority, institutions, and political bodies, each unit of governance is expected to serve and add to the strength of the Union, besides maintaining its own respective identity and integrity.

The Constitution builds the federal Union from local bodies to the states to regional bodies, with a Union government (national government) to coordinate the various structures of shared rule. The central authority has regulatory powers over a fairly large number of subjects. But matters of local import have been devolved to the subnational units. The Constitution does acknowledge the supremacy of the jurisdiction of each federal unit. However, there also exists "differential loading" – some units having more functional responsibilities than the others – within different or similar subject areas. Thus while states' authority over primary education is by and large established, the same does not hold true for higher education, where it has to share its jurisdiction with the central government.

Broadly, the Union government has been assigned the three important roles of: upholding national unity and integrity, maintaining constitutional and political order in the constituent units, and planning of national economic development. States hardly question the constitutional intent and sanction of these powers of the Union government, but they frequently seek procedural transparency and participation in the decision-making process of the Union government, especially regarding the exercise of authority over the second and third roles. They insist on minimal interference from the Union government in the affairs of the states, particularly when it is on the pretext of maintaining constitutional political order within the units. In this regard, they particularly object to the exercise of emergency powers by the Union government under Article 356, which allows for the deployment of military forces, reserving state bills for presidential consideration and approval by the Governor. The common refrain is that the Union government has accumulated and brought within its domain a large number of developmental items, on the pretext of serving larger national and public interests, which could otherwise have belonged to the states. This has resulted in the concentration of high yielding revenue items in the hands of the Union government, and the consequential narrowing of the revenue generating capacity of the states.

For these reasons, the states have been demanding that the authority of the Union government be dramatically reduced. Many high-level commissions have been set up to study the question. All of them, except one, have found the Constitution not only sound but also flexible enough to decentralize powers and authority from the Union government to the regions. They have suggested many functional modifications in the working of Union-state relations. One such Commission on Union-state relations was headed by Justice R. S. Sarkaria which advanced far-reaching recommendations.

In 1990, the government of India set up the Inter-State Council (ISC) to implement the recommendations of the "Sarkaria Commission" and to promote harmonization of inter-state and Union-state relations and policy coordination. The ISC works to seek consensus on the possible changes in the structure and process of inter-state relationships. The ISC has succeeded in developing some agreement on repairing crucial areas of federal relationships. Other councils have been established to build stronger inter-state relations. However, apart from the North-Eastern Council, the other councils are either defunct or riddled with mutual antipathy.

The most recent changes to Indian federalism have been designed to ensure good governance, by enabling private and public partnership at all orders of governance. The good governance agenda is leading to the widening of state autonomy, particularly in the area of economic development. The states are permitted to introduce competitive economic reforms through various forms of political and administrative decentralization. Now the states are able to invite direct foreign investment on their own. They are allowed to introduce reforms and innovations in the state economy, and to decentralize powers according to the individual needs of the concerned states. The federal system has shown enough resilience to adapt, accommodating both the imperatives of national unity and a liberalized market economy of the twenty-first century.

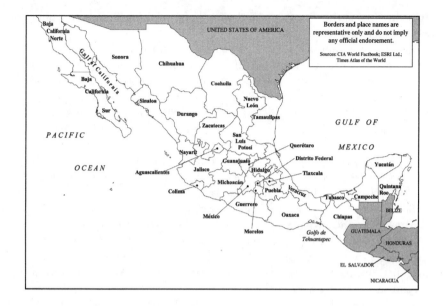

Mexico:
A Historic Election Brings Pressures
for Decentralization

MANUEL GONZÁLEZ OROPEZA

After more than 150 years with a federal system, Mexico has reached a consensus that its highly centralized allocation of powers must be reformed. In response to the historic elections in 2000, the states are seeking more powers in order to foster democracy and pluralism. However, in this dialogue between the federal government and 31 state governments, there is an emerging third party that asks for more autonomy and equality: local governments in the 2,300 munic-ipalities. There are also concerns about the limited status of the Fed-eral District, Mexico City, which encompasses one fifth of the total population of the country.

Despite this general agreement, reform will not be easy, because any changes would need to follow a constitutional amending process. So far, there has been a general lack of will from political actors to make concessions to the rest of the political community. In addition, there has been no agreement on the details of reform, although it is clear that the goal is the reversal of federal powers and increased participation of local governments.

Local governments are generally unprepared to face the challenges posed by this decentralization, with the exception of the big cities. Municipal governments generally lack powers delegated from the state or federal orders of government. Still, they have to solve issues where the confluence of such powers is so intertwined that a clear-cut separation among the different jurisdictions is impossible to make. Unfortunately, the closest order of government to the population, the local government, usually has to respond first on behalf of all the other orders. All municipalities have the same structural institutions, because asymmetry has never existed in Mexican federalism.

Some new state constitutional institutions have been established during these early years of the twenty-first century. The new state constitution of Veracruz (2000) has been a model in this process. However, states that have traditionally relied heavily on federal intervention and institutions have been more reluctant to act independently and in an innovative fashion.

For the federal government, the decentralization process is difficult and painful because it causes an erosion of the federal bureaucracy and a fundamental change in the distribution of fiscal resources. In 2004, there has been a call for a national fiscal convention that will gather all orders of government to discuss how taxation, spending, and fiscal resources will be reformed in the decentralization effort.

The debate on intergovernmental relations has not attracted much attention in Mexico, and so far, the discussion is focused on the more passive federalism of structures rather than the dynamic interaction between all orders of government. Mexico has certainly become more democratic, but it is thanks to the change of political leadership rather than the fundamental reform of institutions.

> Mexico has certainly become more democratic, but it is thanks to the change of political leadership rather than the fundamental reform of institutions.

In other countries, the rigid distribution of powers between federal and state jurisdictions has been eased by the more flexible interpretation of judicial authorities. This has not been the case in Mexico. Judicial intervention has been muted, so the federal constitutional framework will need more deliberate reform. One article of the federal Constitution limits the judicial interpretation of Supreme Court resolutions. However, another article does provide a way to resolve "constitutional controversy," by which any order of government can submit a special controversy before the Supreme Court whenever it considers that another is infringing upon the allocation of powers established in the Constitution.

All federal powers are granted expressly in the Constitution, while the states possess "reserved" powers, not expressed in the Constitution and open to development in their respective constitutions. However, because the federal government has full responsibility for taxation and international affairs, it can levy taxes and make international agreements on any subject it deems appropriate, even on those matters reserved to states. The federal government has also benefited from a catch-all clause in the Constitution, known as the "implied" powers clause, that on rare occasions has been interpreted as an escape from the rigid general rule of the distribution of powers.

On the other hand, most states have not taken advantage of the possibilities of their unspecified reserved powers, by exhibiting self-restraint. One prominent example has been the lack of protection for human rights in the state constitutions. Mexican states have only expanded their own inhabitants' human rights under exceptional circumstances and have rarely provided their own remedies to protect them. Another example of this restraint is the uniformity of state legislatures. All states have so far remained with a unicameral legislature, even though several have proposed a second chamber.

Political conditions in Mexico are ripe for reforming the current system. Opposition parties are all over the political and electoral map and the President does not control the federal Congress as in previous years. The same is true at the state order and proportional representation has introduced plurality in the composition of municipal bodies as well as state legislatures. Most of the state executives are from parties different than the federal executive. As a result, many states have successfully introduced governance changes and have imposed a stronger rule of law in elections.

While the political climate appears to be perfect for change, it also frustrates the quick and long-reaching reform of government institutions. The Senate of the federal Congress is now studying the best ways to decentralize power. It appears that the delegation or legislated transfer of powers from the federal government to the sub-units might work well within Mexico's Civil Law tradition, where judicial intervention restrained.

Observers who used to understand the political realities of Mexico may be surprised to see the new developments on federalism and other political reforms. They may come to realize that the Mexico of today is now under construction.

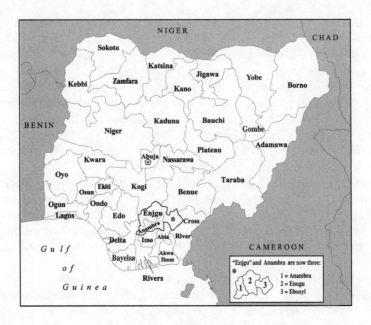

Nigeria: Over-Centralization after Decades of Military Rule

J. ISAWA ELAIGWU

From its independence in 1960 until a new democratic government took office in 1999, Nigeria developed into a highly centralized federal state. The devastating civil war in the late 1960s, followed by decades of military rule, has left most government powers in the hands of the national government. Now, many Nigerians are concerned about over-centralization of powers in a country that has over 400 linguistic-cultural groups and a population estimated at about 130 million, with a high growth rate of 2.6 percent.

Nigeria's federation emerged through a process of conquest and charters granted to British companies from the middle of the nineteenth century, when a variety of nationalities lost their sovereignty to British colonial authority. The amalgamation of various colonial territories gave birth to Nigeria as a colonial state in 1914. The legal system is based on English Common Law, Islamic Sharia (in some northern states), and Customary Law.

The period between 1946 and 1960 saw the gradual federalization of Nigeria until its independence in 1960. Given the heterogeneity of the Nigerian state and mutual suspicions among groups, Nigerian nationalists opted for a federal system of government in the terminal colonial period, as a mechanism for striking necessary compromises. From a federation with a weak federal government in 1960, it had become highly centralized by 1999. A number of factors were responsible for this centralizing trend.

The first is the hierarchical nature of military rule. The military ruled Nigeria for almost thirty years after the civil war. The military command structure was able to centralize powers with minimal resistance from subnational units. Second, the Nigerian civil war in the late 1960s had resulted in a declaration of a state of emergency. Powers which were usurped by the federal government were never returned after the war. Third, the creation of many new subnational states – growing progressively from just three regions to thirty-six states – reduced the resource bases of the states. Fourth, the profit tax on petroleum accrues to the federal government, giving it the vast majority of government revenues. Finally, the need for harmonization in areas of inter-state commerce, international trade, and globalization, has added to the leverage of the federal government in relations with states.

Consequently by May 1999, when a new democratic government took office, there were cries by many political activists about the over-centralization of powers in the federation. The new 1999 Constitution recognizes three tiers of government: federal, state, and local. In the allocation of major policy areas and responsibilities, the Constitution provides an exclusive list of central powers, a concurrent list of shared powers, with all residual powers going to the states, and a fourth list of local government functions.

The exclusive list contains 68 items which include citizenship, immigration, defence, policing, external affairs, mining, nuclear energy, regulation of political parties, and the public debt of the federation. The concurrent list of shared powers includes allocation of revenue, electoral law, universities, technological and post-primary education, scientific and technological research, and industrial, commercial and agricultural development. The local government functions include roads, sewage and refuse disposal, registration of all births, deaths, and marriages, primary, adult and vocational education, agriculture, health services, and any other functions conferred by the State House Assembly.

> Consequently by May 1999, when a new democratic government took office, there were cries by many political activists about the over-centralization of powers in the federation.

In addition to concern about over-centralization, efforts are now un-
derway to streamline intergovernmental relations in the overlapping
areas of jurisdiction. These include security, education, housing, agriculture, health, and water. There are also calls to review the 1999 Constitution, even though it is still relatively new. Another point of
contention is the Nigeria Police Force which is included in the exclusive list. Some states are demanding the right to establish their own
state police forces.

To go along with the powers and responsibilities stipulated in the
Constitution, fiscal and monetary powers are also allocated to each tier
of government. The federal government raises revenues from mining
rents and royalties, the petroleum profits tax, the personal income tax,
import and export duties, and a capital gains tax. State governments
raise revenue from land taxes, estate duties, licence fees, betting, and
sales taxes. Local governments raise revenue from entertainment
taxes, property tax, and trading and marketing licences. As a growing
number of Nigerians demand decentralization of powers, many feel
that the tax powers of each tier of government should be reversed, in
favour of states and local governments.

However, there is a general sense of complacency among the three
orders of government about revenue generation. Each order depends
heavily on statutory allocations from the federal account, which in
turn depends heavily on revenues from petroleum resources. This pat-
tern skews the development priorities of governments. Nigerians who
are concerned about their country's fiscal strength are proposing a
more aggressive revenue generation effort.

Are there challenges for the future? Federalism is brought about by
diversity among various states. Yet the policy in Nigeria is to treat all
the states in the same way. The equal payment of subsidies, salaries,
and other benefits is likely to exacerbate regional economic disparities. The equitable distribution of resources among Nigerian groups
will continue to be difficult. As adjustments take place in the federation, there will certainly be strains and stresses.

Other challenges to Nigeria's federation include providing good
governance, visionary leadership, and a strong economy. Many Nigerian leaders do not accept the benefits of federalism in the country.
Many of the elites see federalism in technical terms and show no
commitment to the values of power sharing that must accompany it.
Nigerian citizens do not yet fully understand democracy and their
Constitution, nor how the rights of citizens must be balanced with
their obligations in the federation. Nigerians will need to find a better
way to work together, before they can move forward.

Spain:
A Unique Model of State Autonomy

XAVIER BERNADÍ GIL
AND CLARA VELASCO

The federal model established by the Spanish Constitution of 1978 is being widely questioned today. All political parties accept the need to reform the Constitution, although there is no agreement on the scope of the reforms. Some states, in Spain named "Autonomous Communities," have begun to make changes to their "Statutes of Autonomy," acts that define the powers and institutions of the constituent entities. Some of these reforms are not only ambitious – especially in Catalonia and in the Basque Country – but also rather controversial.

The Spanish Constitution is unusual in many ways. First, in spite of not being federal in name, the 1978 Constitution carried out a greater decentralization of political powers than exists in many nominally federal countries. The overall structure is known as the "State of the Autonomies" or simply as "the State." The Spanish system has great possibilities for evolution, either through mechanisms that allow changes to the constitutional distribution of powers, or through interpretation of undefined constitutional provisions. The Constitution does not identify any of the Autonomous Communities that constitute the country, nor does it fix their powers, which have been left to subsequent laws. All of these factors justify the assessment that the Spanish model is a "sub-constitutional" model.

Prior to 1978, 40 years of totalitarian dictatorship had solidified the traditional centralism of Spain. However, in that year the country passed from a unitary state to one constituted by seventeen Autonomous Communities, which have significant political, administrative, and financial powers. The adoption of the 1978 Constitution launched the longest period of regional autonomy that Spain has known.

While the practical application of the Constitution, and, in particular, the scope of the powers of the central government, has resulted in extensive autonomy for the Autonomous Communities in quantitative terms, the quality of this autonomy is questionable. The measure of independence is wide, but very thin, and the system has not satisfactorily balanced unity and diversity. Spain is a pluralistic society, having more similarities to the Belgian or the Swiss experience than to the American or the Germanic one. Some territories have a stronger tradition of self-government, with their own language and Civil Law. These communities believe that there is an imposed degree of uniformity they deem excessive, for example, in matters related to local government and public administration.

> In spite of not being federal in name, the 1978 Constitution carried out a greater decentralization of political powers than exists in many nominally federal countries.

The greatest degree of asymmetry between the Autonomous Communities occurs in fiscal affairs. Two Autonomous Communities, the Basque Country and Navarre, enjoy financial privileges due to historical reasons. In some other communities – Catalonia for example – fiscal relations are essentially characterized by an imbalance between public responsibilities and financial resources, since the central government controls not only the main sources of income, but also the management of the financial system. The latter is scarcely defined in the Constitution.

The Constitution enumerates the central government's powers, but it does not determine the powers of the Autonomous Communities. These are defined by the Autonomous Communities' Statutes of Autonomy, thereby fulfilling an almost constitutional function, with the only limit being those powers reserved to the State. The number and degree of powers can vary among the Autonomous Communities, although the current level of powers is roughly equal for most of them.

Although the Spanish system is based on the exclusivity of powers, in many cases powers are shared. On some occasions, the central government enacts legislation and the Autonomous Communities are required to develop and execute it. All residual powers belong to the State, although it may transfer or delegate part of its powers to the Autonomous Communities. The lack of definition of some key aspects of the allocation of powers, as well as the shortage of mechanisms promoting institutional relations, has resulted in a great many cases brought before the Constitutional Court.

The current model faces other important challenges. The Autonomous Communities complain that they have very little influence within the central institutions of the State and their decision-making processes. Unfortunately, the Senate has failed to function as a chamber of territorial representation, even though the Constitution formally attributes it that role. Integration into the European Union in 1986 increased the problems derived from this participative deficit. The yielding of sovereignty to European institutions is affecting not only the powers of the State, but also those of the Autonomous Communities. The Communities have no important role in decision-making processes related to European matters, nor do they have direct representation before European institutions.

Globalization has affected the balance of powers in other ways. The exclusive State power in immigration was never considered a problem until it obliged the Autonomous Communities, who are responsible for such services of the welfare-state as health, education, and housing, to assume important political and financial responsibilities in a field in which they have no political authority. A similar situation is occurring in the case of information and communication technologies, growing fields whose political repercussions were not considered by the Constitution. The guarantee and stability of the financing system, as well as the adaptation of the judicial system to the compound structure of the country, are other important problems that have not still been resolved.

The Constitution of 1978 has allowed Spain to pass from a unitary and centralized State to a new arrangement that resembles other federal systems. After a process of consensus-seeking, the result was transcribed into an open and flexible constitutional text. However, developments since then have caused reason for much debate among sectors that have very different interpretations of the system. The current political scene suggests that instead of repairing the "breakdowns" of the system, perhaps Spain will decide to replace it entirely.

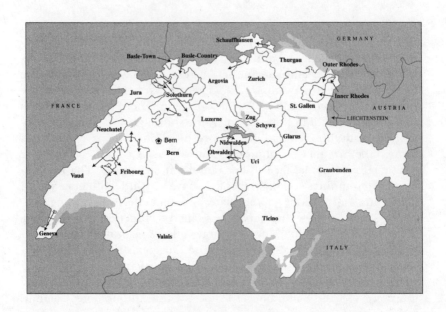

Switzerland:
Seeking a Balance between
Shared Rule and Self-Rule

SARAH BYRNE AND THOMAS FLEINER

Switzerland is a notably decentralized federation that employs several constitutional devices to resist any shift of powers to the central government. While most federal countries have shown a tendency to centralize in response to globalization, cantonal and local governments in Switzerland still control the majority of government expenditures and can influence important national policy decisions. Now the cantons are experimenting with cooperative federalism, in order to participate in the decision-making processes of the federal government.

Switzerland, a country with four official languages and two historically conflicting religious communities, adopted its federal constitution in 1848, after a civil war. It became the second federation to come into existence, strongly influenced by American federalism. The federal constitution was a compromise, between liberals promoting a unitary state and conservatives defending the former confederation. The cantons maintained their original autonomy, now as "self-rule" within a federation, and shared their sovereignty with the federation. Sensitive issues such as culture, language, education, and the relationship between state and religion remained under cantonal jurisdiction, while respecting the federal constitutional entitlement to freedom of religion. With this system, the small consensus-driven democracy was able to develop peacefully from a rural society into a highly diversified modern state. Even now, in a globalized economy, cantonal and local governments still control two-thirds of government revenue and public expenditures.

> With this system, the small consensus-driven democracy was able to develop peacefully from a rural society into a highly diversified modern state.

The federal government is responsible for national defence, citizenship rights and immigration law, civil and criminal law, economic development, currency, national transport and communication. Cantons, in turn, are responsible for important parts of public order and policing, education, welfare, health, and regional and local planning. Despite shifts in the past 150 years, the guiding principle of the distribution of powers and responsibilities remains that of "subsidiarity." This means that tasks will only be assigned to the federal government if it can perform them more efficiently than at the cantonal order. Furthermore, the federal government should only use its powers if it can do so more efficiently than the cantonal order. The rest shall be left to the cantons to perform.

The assignment of responsibilities to different orders of government, each of which act independently, effectively prevents the concentration of state power in the hands of one institution. The division of responsibilities is known as "self-rule," because each order of government acts independently. Article 3 of the federal Constitution contains the basic principle of self-rule in Switzerland: all areas of jurisdiction are cantonal, unless otherwise stated within the federal Constitution. For the majority of federal powers and responsibilities, the federal government does not provide the administration to put the law into action. However, federal laws are binding for all government agencies, regardless whether they are cantonal or federal. Therefore, the cantons must apply federal law, and in case of disagreement, federal law is superior to cantonal law.

Nevertheless, many federal laws expressly reserve large areas of jurisdiction to the cantons. Due to the diversity among cantons with respect to size, geography, and demographics, as well as the multicultural character of the population, it is nearly impossible for the federal government to take the distinctiveness of each canton into account, unless it grants them broad discretion. Even within federal jurisdiction, the cantons can adopt the application of the law to their local conditions, considering local cultural distinctiveness. This is an important factor in a country with as much cultural diversity as Switzerland.

Self-rule alone is usually not enough, because of the centralizing influence of many political domains such as foreign policy, environmental protection, and security. Therefore, the cantons have another instrument they can use to control central power: "shared rule." For certain policy decisions, the central power depends on the approval of the cantons, whether expressed directly through their governments, through popular referenda, or through other means of representation. For instance, foreign policy is a federal responsibility in Switzerland, but for important treaties, the federal government must consult the cantonal governments and take their opinions into consideration before signing an agreement. In the areas where the cantons have yielded jurisdiction to the federal government, they can effectively control the federal decision-making process through the institutions providing shared rule.

A process of centralization has gradually diminished cantonal autonomy, even though powers are not easily transferred from one order to another. In a system of semi-direct democracy, amendments to the Constitution must be approved in a referendum. Citizens are often reluctant to hand more powers to the federal government, because of greater democratic accountability at the local order than at the national order. Still, since 1874, approximately 140 constitutional amendments have shifted some of the cantons' extensive powers to the federal order. Compared to the earlier constitutions, the Constitution of 1999 puts more emphasis on the principle of shared rule than on the principle of self-rule. Surprisingly, this has not led to a strengthening of the second chamber of parliament, in which the cantons are represented. Instead, the shared rule principle has been implemented by cantonal executive bodies taking a more direct role in the decision-making processes of the federal government. This cooperative federalism is a new and creative development, which may lead Switzerland to more effective decision making and greater flexibility.

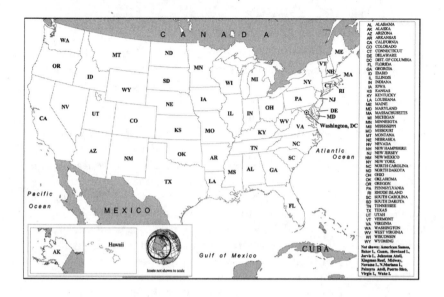

AL	ALABAMA
AK	ALASKA
AZ	ARIZONA
AR	ARKANSAS
CA	CALIFORNIA
CO	COLORADO
CT	CONNECTICUT
DE	DELAWARE
DC	DIST. OF COLUMBIA
FL	FLORIDA
GA	GEORGIA
ID	IDAHO
IL	ILLINOIS
IN	INDIANA
IA	IOWA
KS	KANSAS
KY	KENTUCKY
LA	LOUISIANA
ME	MAINE
MD	MARYLAND
MA	MASSACHUSETTS
MI	MICHIGAN
MN	MINNESOTA
MS	MISSISSIPPI
MO	MISSOURI
MT	MONTANA
NE	NEBRASKA
NV	NEVADA
NH	NEW HAMPSHIRE
NJ	NEW JERSEY
NM	NEW MEXICO
NY	NEW YORK
NC	NORTH CAROLINA
ND	NORTH DAKOTA
OH	OHIO
OK	OKLAHOMA
OR	OREGON
PA	PENNSYLVANIA
RI	RHODE ISLAND
SC	SOUTH CAROLINA
SD	SOUTH DAKOTA
TN	TENNESSEE
TX	TEXAS
UT	UTAH
VT	VERMONT
VA	VIRGINIA
WA	WASHINGTON
WV	WEST VIRGINIA
WI	WISCONSIN
WY	WYOMING

Not shown: American Samoa, Baker I., Guam, Howland I., Jarvis I., Johnston Atoll, Kingman Reef, Midway, Navassa I., N.Mariana I., Palmyra Atoll, Puerto Rico, Virgin I., Wake I.

Insets not shown to scale

The United States of America: A Federal Government of Limited Powers

ELLIS KATZ

International developments are having a significant impact on the ways in which all governments function and the United States is no exception. Global trade agreements, the demand for human rights, and even the fight against international terrorism have all created increasing pressures to centralize government responsibilities. For the United States, these pressures are causing new changes to American federalism, which is at the heart of its constitutional structure.

American federalism is a delegation of limited powers and responsibilities to the federal government, with all other powers reserved for the states. The original American states were fully functioning constitutional bodies before the writing and ratification of the Constitution. After declaring their independence from the United Kingdom in 1776, eleven of the thirteen states discarded their colonial charters and adopted constitutions, providing both for the structure and operation of government and for the protection of individual rights. The states were also linked together as a confederation under the Articles of Confederation. However, when that limited union proved inadequate to meet the international and economic challenges of the post-independence years, the states sent delegates to a constitutional convention to, in the words of the Constitution, "create a more perfect union."

The more perfect union established by the United States Constitution of 1788 creates a more powerful federal government, with a bicameral legislature, a strong chief executive, and a Supreme Court. At the same time, the Constitution vests the federal government with limited, albeit very important powers that it did not have under the Articles of Confederation, including the power to tax and spend for the public welfare, and the power to regulate interstate and foreign commerce. All powers not delegated to the federal government are reserved to the states, exactly where they were before the Constitution was written and ratified.

This distribution of responsibilities, which left the states almost wholly responsible for domestic affairs, has changed over time. Sometimes it has changed by formal constitutional amendment, but more often by broad interpretations of federal power under the taxing and spending clause and the interstate and foreign commerce clause by the Supreme Court of the United States. The Fourteenth Amendment, adopted in 1868 after the American Civil War, gave the federal government a major role to play in the protection of rights. The Sixteenth Amendment, adopted in 1913, enhanced the federal government's power to tax incomes, allowing it to develop a system of grants-in-aid that now exceeds $600 billion and affects almost every area of domestic policy. The United States Supreme Court has interpreted the reach of federal authority very broadly under both the taxing and spending and interstate and foreign commerce clauses. This permits the federal government to regulate almost all forms of economic activity and financially support a wide variety of domestic projects. Since the mid-1990s, there have been a few decisions by the Supreme Court that limit federal authority and remind us that the federal government is a government of limited powers. However it remains to be seen whether these decisions will serve as a real brake on the expansion of federal authority.

One effect of the expansion of federal activity in domestic policy has been the creation of a complex web of intergovernmental relationships in which local, state, and federal authorities bargain with each other in both the making and implementation of public policy. This development is often referred to as cooperative federalism. Some commentators maintain that the federal government has become so dominant in its bargaining position that cooperative federalism has been replaced by a kind of coercive federalism, in which the federal government increasingly preempts state laws, encroaches on state tax bases, and compels the states to comply with federal policies.

Historic, social, and economic forces have shaped American federalism over the past 200 years – the purchase of the Louisiana Territory from France in 1803, the subsequent opening of the American west, the Civil War, the constitutional amendments adopted in its aftermath, industrialization, immigration and urbanization, the Great Depression and President Franklin D. Roosevelt's New Deal programs of the 1930s, and the Second World War and the Cold War that followed it. While these events increased the role of the federal government in the American federal system, all governments – federal, state, and local – do more than they did 200 years ago. Increasingly, policies are not in the exclusive domain of any one government, but involve cooperation among all orders of government.

> Increasingly, policies are not in the exclusive domain of any one government, but involve cooperation among all orders of government.

Today, globalization, international terrorism, and the demand for human rights are likely to affect American federalism in much the same ways, with the power of the federal government increasing and further momentum towards cooperative federalism. For example, the United States is a signatory of both the North American Free Trade Agreement (NAFTA) and the General Agreement on Tariffs and Trade (GATT). These trade agreements are binding international agreements, which the United States must fulfill regardless of its internal political arrangements. Consequently, the United States Supreme Court could declare state regulations invalid, not because they violate the United States Constitution, but because they violate international agreements.

The federal role in law enforcement has increased because of the threat of international terrorism. This enhanced federal role will not replace local law enforcement; in fact, local responsibilities will also increase. It does mean, however, that law enforcement, like most other governmental functions, will increasingly become a shared responsibility and will pose new challenges to American patterns of cooperative federalism. Finally, the worldwide demand for human rights places new pressures on state practices, such as capital punishment, which, while not violating the United States Constitution, are often perceived as violating international norms.

Comparative Reflections

RONALD L. WATTS

A constitutional distribution of legislative and executive authority and finances among the general and constituent unit governments has constituted a fundamental, indeed defining, aspect in the design and operation of these federations. But while a constitutional distribution of authority, responsibilities and finances among the orders of government has been a fundamental feature common to them, there has been an enormous variation in the constitutional form and scope and in the operation of the distribution of powers in different federations.

Different geographic, historical, economic, security, demographic, linguistic, cultural, intellectual and international factors have affected the strength of the common interests and of diversity peculiar to each federation. Consequently, the specific distribution of authority and the degree of noncentralization has varied among federations.

Among differences in the *form* of the constitutional distribution of authority have been the extent to which the exclusivity or concurrent jurisdiction of governments has been emphasized, the assignment of state or provincial powers by a specific listing of jurisdiction or by a general allocation of residual authority, the extent to which the assignment of executive responsibilities coincides with or is differentiated from legislative jurisdiction, the symmetry or asymmetry in the powers assigned to different constituent units, the formal constitutional recognition or not of local governments as a third constitutional order of government guaranteed their own self-government, and the extent of federal overriding and emergency powers. In terms of the *scope* of constitutional powers, there have been considerable differences in the relative roles of government in different policy areas. The financial arrangements and the degree of reliance upon intergovernmental financial transfers has also varied. As a result, there has been substantial variation the degrees of centralization and non-centralization and of intergovernmental cooperation or competition among governments within different federations.

Within each federation there has in practice been considerable difference between the constitutional form and the operational reality of the distribution of powers. In most cases political practice and processes have transformed the way the constitution has operated. A key factor here has been the impact of political party and interest group activities affecting political bargaining and compromises.

While in each federation there has been a constitutional allocation of specific powers to each government, overlaps and intergovernmental interdependence have proved inevitable and unavoidable in every federation. As a result this has usually required a variety of processes and institutions to facilitate intergovernmental collaboration. But here too there has been considerable variation among federations in the degree and character of intergovernmental collaboration and in the balance struck between the independence and interdependence of governments. For instance, Germany and Mexico are marked by closely interlocked relationships while Canada and Belgium in comparative terms lean to the other extreme.

Federations have not been static organizations and over time the distribution of powers in each has had to adapt and evolve to respond to changing needs and circumstances and to the development of new issues and policy areas. In seeking a balance between rigidity to protect regional and minority interests, on the one hand, and the need to respond effectively to changing circumstances, on the other, a number of processes have played an important role, although in varying degrees in different federations. These have included formal constitutional amendments, judicial interpretation and review, intergovernmental financial adjustments, and intergovernmental collaboration and agreements. The evolution of the distribution of powers in response to changing conditions has over time in some instances, such as the United States, Australia, Germany, Brazil, Mexico and Nigeria, displayed a general trend to the reinforcement and expansion of federal powers. But this has not been a universal trend. Canada, India, and Belgian have instead over time experienced a trend to greater decentralization reflecting the strength of the diverse communities composing them.

Virtually all contemporary federations are currently experiencing pressures and debates for adjustments to their distribution of powers in order to meet changing and new conditions. The present context of globalization and regional integration, of membership of federations in such supra-federal organizations as the European Union or NAFTA, of emphasis upon market economies and the benefits of economic decentralization, and of concerns about security from terrorism, are all requiring a rebalancing of centralization and noncentralization and of collaborative and competitive federalism. With this has gone recognition that federations and the distribution of responsibilities in them should not be conceived as rigid structures but as evolving processes enabling the continuous reconciliation of internal diversity within their overarching federal frameworks. In this respect the distribution of powers and responsibilities within all these federations and the balance between "shared rule" through common institutions on the one hand and "self-rule" for the constituent units on the other may be typified in the words of Richard Simeon's chapter as a continuing "work in progress."

Glossary

ADMINISTRATIVE DECENTRALIZATION   downward or outward transfer (devolution) of administrative powers and responsibilities within or between levels of government.

ADMINISTRATIVE FEDERALISM   term given to German-style federalism whereby the division of powers is not primarily between specified policy domains (as in US-style legislative federalism) but between the legislative authority concentrated at the national level, and the responsibility for implementation and administration at the sub-national level.

ARTICLES OF CONFEDERATION (AND PERPETUAL UNION)   first constitution of the United States of America, 1781–88.

ASYMMETRICAL FEDERALISM   denotes unequal or non-identical distribution of powers and responsibilities among the constituent units of a federal system.

AUTONOMOUS COMMUNITIES   the 17 component units of the Spanish state; created under the 1978 democratic constitution but not technically constituent units.

BASIC LAW   literal translation of *Grundgesetz*; the constitution of the Federal Republic of Germany.

BASQUE COUNTRY   one of the four "historic communities" that led Spain's process of federalization through devolution of powers to the 17 regional Autonomous Communities.

BIPARTISAN   action that involves agreement between the main opposed parties of a political system.

BIPOLARITÉ   bipolarity; reference to the fact that Belgium is a country whose constitutional politics are dominated by the tensions between two main language communities.

CANBERRA   the national capital of the Commonwealth of Australia, located in the Australian Capital Territory (ACT); informal reference in Australia to the national government.

CANTON   name for the 26 constituent units in the Swiss federation.

CATALONIA   one of the four "historic communities" that led Spain's process of federalization through devolution of powers to the 17 regional Autonomous Communities.

CHIEF EXECUTIVE   informal term for the person who occupies the combined position of head of government and head of state in a presidential system of government.

COERCIVE FEDERALISM   see co-operative federalism.

COLLABORATIVE FEDERALISM   see co-operative federalism

COMMERCE POWER/CLAUSE   one of Congress's enumerated powers under Article I, section 8 of the US Constitution, the power "To regulate Commerce with foreign Nations, and among the several States ...". Primary constitutional basis for the centralization of American federalism.

COMMISSION COMMUNAUTAIRE FRANÇAISE   the sub-national authority in Belgium of the French-speaking community; responsibility for a range of non-territorial cultural and social functions.

COMMON LAW   British tradition of a legal system based on accumulated judicial decisions known as precedent and diffused through the English-speaking world. Contrast with statute or civil code law; see civil law.

COMMUNE   self-governing towns and cities; term for major component of the third order of government in some federations (Belgium, Switzerland).

COMPETITIVE FEDERALISM   the idea that the constituent governments of a federation should compete with each other in offering their own range of public services and tax structures to enhance overall socio-economic efficiency and effectiveness.

COMPLEMENTARY LAWS   type of legislation requiring a special quorum in the Brazilian legislature; in lieu of formal constitutional amendments.

CONCURRENT POWERS   An approach to dividing powers whereby levels of government are implicitly or explicitly expected to share jurisdiction over specific policy areas. Can be effected either by creating a list of shared powers, or by granting authority over various functions to one level of government without providing for those powers to be exclusive.

CONSENSUS DEMOCRACY   a democracy where culture and institutions are oriented toward multi-party governance and the negotiated settlement of disagreements in preference to the more winner-take-all approach of adversarial majoritarian systems.

CONSTITUTIONAL   establishment of the system of government on a firm basis of legal rules regulating and limiting the exercise of power.

CONSTITUTIONAL CONVENTION   1. a specially convened meeting of representatives to draft or enact fundamental law.   2. an unwritten rule of constitutional practice.

CONSTITUTIONAL COURT   a judicial body exercising final jurisdiction specifically over constitutional questions including the relationship between levels of government in a federation, as distinct from a "supreme court" or one that acts as the apex of the legal system in general. First established in Austria; examples now include Belgium's Court of Arbitration (*Cour d'arbitrage*) and Germany's Federal Constitutional Court (*Bundesverfassungsgericht*) and the constitutional courts of South Africa and the Russian Federation.

COOPERATIVE FEDERALISM practice and principle of modern federalism whereby the levels of government work together to coordinate policy design and delivery in areas of overlapping responsibility. Prescribed in some federations (e.g., Germany's "joint tasks") but more typically an adaptive response of governments to the realities of modern federal governance. Does not necessarily entail an equality of power and resources between the participating levels of government and indeed may represent an exercise in COERCIVE FEDERALISM whereby the superior resources or powers of the central government allow it to impose uniform policies.

COUNCIL the legislative branch of community and regional government in Belgium.

CUSTOMARY LAW long-standing unwritten legal norms of traditional societies where no formal legal system or judicial organs existed.

DECENTRALIZATION shift of power from central or national government to the sub-national governments of a federation.

DELEGATED POWERS powers that are granted by one level of government to another on a revocable basis (though the term is sometimes used loosely to denote simply the granting of powers to a particular body).

DEVOLUTION OF POWERS transfer of powers and responsibilities from a central government to subordinate entities; not necessarily based on constitutional change.

DIFFERENTIAL LOADING varying degree of completeness with which a level of government exercises authority over a particular policy domain.

DIRECT DEMOCRACY involvement of the citizenry in law-making as an alternative or supplement to government by elected representatives; notably in Switzerland through ratification of legislation and constitutional amendments by referendums or initiation of legislation by popular action; also "semi-direct" as indication that it complements, not supersedes, representative democracy.

DUE PROCESS the core requirement of the principle of the rule of law that authoritative actions must be in conformity with stipulated legal procedures guaranteeing justice.

EQUALIZATION formal redistribution of revenues within a federation to provide a minimum standard of resourcing across jurisdictions and thereby ensure citizens a comparable level of government services regardless of their place of residence. Also "horizontal fiscal equalization" (HFE).

ENUMERATED POWERS authority to legislate over specific matters explicitly assigned to a particular level or levels of government by the constitution; see residual powers for contrast.

EXCLUSIVE POWERS/JURISDICTION   powers allocated solely to one level of government in a federal system either by identification in those terms or by a clause that prohibits their exercise by other levels of government; see concurrent powers for contrast.

FEDERAL ACCOUNT   the consolidated revenue of the national government of Nigeria.

FEDERAL CONSTITUTIONAL COURT   see constitutional court.

FEDERAL CONGRESS   *Congreso de la Unión*; the bicameral national legislature of Mexico's presidential system of government; also translated as Congress of the Union.

FEDERAL COUNCIL   the upper house or second chamber of the bicameral national legislature of the Russian Federation.

FEDERAL GOVERNMENT   colloquial and sometimes official term for the national government of a federation.

FEDERAL LOYALTY   requirement of the German constitution that the country must be governed in conformity with principles of federalism.

FEDERATION   1. a form of government in which powers are constitutionally divided among two or more orders of government; typically a federal state. 2. the process of forming such a government.

FEDERATIVE DEMOCRACIES   democratic federations.

FISCAL EQUILIBRIUM   balance between revenue needs and revenue resources across the different levels of government in a federation.

FLEMISH   the Dutch-speaking community in Belgium.

FRAMEWORK JURISDICTION   authority of the national government in Germany to establish overarching policy standards in particular areas where the responsibility otherwise lies with the *Länder* (States).

FRENCH-LANGUAGE COMMUNITY COMMISSION   see *Commission communautaire française.*

GOVERNMENT   specifically used for the executive branch of community and region authorities in Belgium.

GREAT DEPRESSION   the economic depression that gripped the advanced industrial world for a decade from the New York Stock Market crash of October 1929 until the onset of the Second World War.

HARMONIZATION   establishment of comparability in rules and regulations between constituent units of a political order as an alternative to uniformity.

IMPLIED POWERS   powers not explicitly granted in the constitution but necessarily or logically arising from other powers; may or may not be supported by an implied powers clause such as the "necessary and proper" clause of the US Constitution.

INDUSTRIAL RELATIONS   legal and economic relationship between employers and employees in the workplace.

INTERGOVERNMENTAL RELATIONS   relations between the governments of sub-national units or between various orders of governments for the purpose of policy co-ordination and/or agreement on shared programs etc.

INTER-STATE   relations between member states of a federation.

JAMMU AND KASHMIR   the only state in the Indian Union with its own constitution rather than one outlined in the Union Constitution.

JOINT RESPONSIBILITIES   concurrent powers under the German constitution.

JOINT TAXES   tax sources that a constitution stipulates shall be shared by the two levels of government; notably in Germany.

JUDICIAL INTERPRETATION   role of the courts in establishing precise meaning of constitutional provisions or legislative acts.

JURISDICTIONAL IMMUNITY   a constitutional principle in Belgium aiming at the exclusive assignment of powers at both levels of government; see watertight compartments.

LEVELS OF GOVERNMENT   see orders of government.

MULTI-LEVEL GOVERNANCE   distribution of responsibilities and co-ordination of action vertically between a range of governments from local to regional to national.

MUNICIPALITIES   local government of towns or cities; the lowest or third order of government in a federation.

NATIONAL STANDARDS   rules or regulations imposed or applying uniformly across a federation with no scope for variation by the sub-national governments.

NEW DEAL   the slogan of the US Democratic Party under the leadership of Franklin Delano Roosevelt in the 1930s and the umbrella term for the program of economic and social reform launched by the Roosevelt Democrats to counteract the unemployment, deflation, and human suffering of the Great Depression.

NORTH AMERICAN FREE TRADE AGREEMENT (NAFTA)   a set of bilateral treaties establishing the rules for a free trade relationship between Canada, the United States, and Mexico.

ORDERS OF GOVERNMENT   the various levels of government in a federation; typically one overarching central government, several broad regional governments that are the constituent units, and a multitude of local governments, notably municipalities; however, may be more complex (e.g., Russia).

ORIGINAL STATES   those constituent units of a federation that pre-existed the union and were instrumental in its formation.

OVERLAPPING JURISDICTION   sharing of powers and responsibilities over any given policy domain between levels of government.

POLITICAL PLURALITY   free operation of a full range of interests and expression in a political system.

PRIVY COUNCIL   the Judicial Committee of the Privy Council (JCPC) in the United Kingdom; final court of appeal for the British Empire and subsequently British Commonwealth of Nations. Technically not a court but an advisory body to the Crown. Appeal right varied under constitutions and systems of law of the different Dominions, from full in Canada to non-existent in post-independence India; now fully terminated in Australia and Canada.

PROPORTIONAL REPRESENTATION   electoral system that assigns seats in a legislature in a way that provides an accurate reflection of the share of votes received by the contesting parties; effected through nation-wide or regional multi-member electoral districts. Also: PR.

PROVINCE   name for constituent units, as an alternative to states, in various federations (Canada, 10 provinces; South Africa, 9 provinces); in some federations used for divisions below the level of the constituent units (e.g., Spain).

REPUBLIC   1. a system of government where rule is carried out by those directly or indirectly elected by the people; 2. used in Australia to denote constitutional status following proposed replacement of the existing dual regal and vice-regal head of state with an office of a directly or indirectly elected president.

REPUBLICAN FEDERALISM   refers to a democratic system where political power is exercised by those directly or indirectly elected by the people, including the head of state (e.g., Brazil).

RESIDUAL POWERS   those unidentified powers that are left by a federal constitution either implicitly or explicitly to a particular order of government in contrast to explicitly assigned enumerated powers; also reserved powers.

RESERVED POWERS   see residual powers.

REVENUE SHARING   arrangements for the distribution of revenues between levels of government in a federation; typically sub-constitutional but sometimes constitutionally specified.

SELF-RULE   principle of self-government for the constituent units of a in a federation.

SEMI-DIRECT DEMOCRACY   see direct democracy.

SENATE   name of the upper house or second chamber in the bicameral national legislatures of Australia, Belgium, Brazil, Canada, Nigeria, Mexico, and United States of America.

SHARED RULE   principle in Switzerland that certain central government decisions are subject to approval by subnational authorities or by the people.

SPANISH CONSTITUTION OF 1978   democratic constitution after the end of the Franco dictatorship.

STATE HOUSE OF ASSEMBLY   the unicameral State legislature in Nigeria's 36 constituent units.

STATE OF THE AUTONOMIES   de facto (or quasi-) federal structure of the Spanish state resulting from the statutory establishment of the 17 Autonomous Communities under the democratic constitution of 1978.

STATE   1.Term the constituent units in the federations of Australia (6 states), Brazil (26 states), India (28 states), Mexico (31 states), Nigeria (36 states), United States of America (50 states); also informal English language reference to the German *Länder* (singular: *Land*). 2. Term for the polity as a whole used in such federations as Belgium, South Africa, and Spain.

STATUTORY AUTHORITY   established by statute, or Act of the legislature.

SUB-CONSTITUTIONAL   rules and institutional arrangements that may have the force of law but of ordinary (legislative Acts) rather than constitutional law.

SUBSIDIARITY   principle according to which a every task should be left to the lowest level of governance that can perform it effectively.

SUPREME COURT   the highest court for constitutional and other law in Canada, India, Mexico, Nigeria, and the United States.

TAXING AND SPENDING CLAUSE   the opening clause of Article I, section 8 of the US Constitution listing the powers of Congress: "That Congress shall have Power To lay and collect Taxes, Duties Imposts and Excises, to pay the Debts and provide for the common Defence and general welfare of the United States ..." Ambiguity about the scope of the spending power it mandates has made this a contentious clause.

UNITARY STATE   a state with a single centre of sovereign political authority as opposed to a federal state; can be centralized or decentralized but sub-national regional or local governments do not enjoy constitutionally protected status.

WALLOON   the French-speaking community in Belgium.

WATERTIGHT COMPARTMENTS   notion that a division of powers could be drawn that would allow each level of government to exercise authority in its own separate sphere without overlap or conflict with other levels of government in the federation; associated with federal design of the eighteenth and nineteenth centuries.

WESTMINSTER SYSTEM   the version of parliamentary government originating in England, subsequently the United Kingdom. Characterized by evolution of an uncodified constitution and the consolidation of a unitary state; the rule of parliamentary supremacy or sovereignty; absence of judicial review; a strong reliance on unwritten constitutional rules known as conventions, most notably the conventions of responsible cabinet government; the retention of a monarchical head of state exercising only vestigial constitutional power; and the use of the plurality-based single-member electoral system ("first-past-the-post").

Contributors

XAVIER BERNADÍ GIL, senior lecturer of law, Universitat Pompeu Fabra, Barcelona, Spain

RAOUL BLINDENBACHER, vice president, Forum of Federations, Canada / Switzerland

SARAH BYRNE, researcher, Institut du Fédéralisme, Université de Fribourg, Switzerland

HUGUES DUMONT, dean of the faculty of law and director, Fonds National de la Recherche Scientifique, Facultés universitaires Saint-Louis, Brussels, Belgium

J. ISAWA ELAIGWU, president, Institute of Governance and Social Research, Jos, Nigeria and professor emeritus of Political Science at the University of Jos

THOMAS FLEINER, director, Institut du Fédéralisme, and professor of Constitutional and Administrative Law, Université de Fribourg, Switzerland

MANUEL GONZÁLEZ OROPEZA, professor of law, Universidad Nacional Autónoma de México, Mexico City, Mexico

ELLIS KATZ, professor emeritus of political science, Temple University, Philadelphia, United States of America

NICOLAS LAGASSE, researcher, Facultés universitaires Saint-Louis and parliamentary assistant with the Belgian House of Representatives, Brussels, Belgium

CLEMENT MACINTYRE, senior lecturer in politics, University of Adelaide, Australia

GEORGE MATHEW, founding director, Institute of Social Sciences, New Delhi, India

ABIGAIL OSTIEN, communications coordinator, Global Dialogue Program, Forum of Federations, Canada

MARCELO PIANCASTELLI DE SIQUEIRA, director for Public Finance and Regional Studies, Institute for Applied Economic Research, Brasilia, Brazil

HANS-PETER SCHNEIDER, professor emeritus, Institut für Föderalismusforschung, Universität Hannover, Germany

RICHARD SIMEON, professor of political science and law, University of Toronto, Canada

MARC VAN DER HULST, head of the Legal Service of the Belgian House of Representatives and lecturer, constitutional law, Vrije Universiteit Brussel, Belgium

SÉBASTIEN VAN DROOGHENBROECK, researcher, Fonds National de la Recherche Scientifique and lecturer, constitutional and human rights law, Facultés universitaires Saint-Louis, Brussels, Belgium

CLARA VELASCO, researcher, Universitat Pompeu Fabra, Barcelona, Spain

RONALD L. WATTS, principal emeritus and professor emeritus of political studies, Queen's University, Kingston, Canada

JOHN WILLIAMS, reader in Law, Australian National University, Canberra, Australia

Participating Experts

We gratefully acknowledge the input of the following experts who participated in the theme of Distribution of Powers and Responsibilities in Federal Countries. While participants contributed their knowledge and experience, they are in no way responsible for the contents of this booklet.

Ursula Abderhalden, Bundesamt für Justiz, Switzerland
Eleael Acevedo Velásquez, Congreso del Estado de Morelos, Mexico
Christy Adokwu, Benue State Government, Nigeria
José Rosas Aispuro Torres, Ayuntamiento de Durango, Mexico
Fareed Amin, Government of Ontario, Canada
Carlos Araújo Leonetti, Universidade Federal de Santa Catarina, Brazil
Glauco Arbix, Instituto de Pesquisa Econômica Aplicada, Brazil
Enric Argullol, Universitat Pompeu Fabra, Spain
Balveer Arora, Jawaharlal Nehru University, India
Solomon Asemota, Alliance for Democracy, Nigeria
Fabricio Augusto de Oliveira, Brazil
Luis Aureliano Andrade, Universidade Federal de Minas Gerais, Brazil
Carlos Báez Silva, Poder Judicial de la Federación, Mexico
Earl M. Baker, Pennsylvania State Senate (former), United States
John Bannon, Government of South Australia (former), Australia
Javier Barnés, Universidad de Huelva, Spain
José Barragán Barragán, Instituto Federal Electoral, Mexico
Martín Bassols, Congreso de los Diputados, Spain
Antoni Bayona, Generalitat de Catalunya (former), Spain
Isabel Benzo, Presidencia del Gobierno, Spain
Xavier Bernadí Gil, Universitat Pompeu Fabra, Spain
Teresa Bhattacharya, Government of Karnataka (former), India
Raoul Blindenbacher, Forum of Federations, Switzerland/Canada
Thomas Bombois, Université Catholique de Louvain, Belgium

Paul Boothe, University of Alberta, Canada
Raphael Born, Université Catholique de Louvain, Belgium
Francisco Borrás Marimon, Instituto Nacional de Administración Pública, Spain
Albert Breton, University of Toronto, Canada
César Camacho Quiroz, Senado de la República, Mexico
Ronaldo Camillo, Governo do Brasil, Brazil
Gilson Cantarino, Governo do Estado do Rio de Janeiro, Brazil
Beniamino Caravita de Toritto, Osservatorio sul Federalismo e i processi di governo, Italy
Pran Chopra, Centre for Policy Research, India
Sujit Choudhry, University of Toronto, Canada
David Cienfuegos Salgado, Poder Judicial de la Federacion, Mexico
Jan Clement, Raad van State, Belgium
Fabiano Core, Governo do Brazil, Brazil
Luis Cosculluela, Universidad Complutense Madrid, Spain
Sulamis Dain, Universidade Federal do Estado do Rio de Janeiro, Brazil
Rui de Britto Álvares, Fundação do Desenvolvimento Administrativo, Brazil
Pierre-Olivier De Broux, Facultés Universitaires Saint-Louis, Belgium
Armand de Mestral, McGill University, Canada
Jean-Thierry Debry, Université de Liège, Belgium
Xavier Delgrange, Conseil d'État, Belgium
Donald Dennison, Forum of Federations, Canada
Hugues Dumont, Facultés Universitaires Saint-Louis, Belgium
Richard Eckermann, Bezirksregierung Lüneburg, Niedersachsen, Germany
Maureen Egbuna, Intercellular Nigerian Limited, Nigeria
J. Isawa Elaigwu, Institute of Governance and Social Research, Nigeria
Robert Ezeife, Association of Local Government of Nigeria, Nigeria
Patrick Fafard, Government of Canada, Canada
Jeffrey Featherstone, Center for Sustainable Communities, United States
Alexander C. Fischer, Universität Heidelberg, Germany
Thomas Fleiner, Université de Fribourg, Switzerland
Michel Frédérick, Governement du Québec, Canada
Bernie Funston, Northern Canada Consulting, Canada
Peter Gahan, Government of Victoria, Australia
Habu Galadima, University of Jos, Nigeria
Juan Carlos Gómez Martínez, Tribunal Superior de Justicia del Distrito Federal, Mexico
Juan Luis González Alcántara y Carrancá, Tribunal Superior de Justicia del Distrito Federal, Mexico
Manuel Gonzalez Oropeza, Universidad Nacional Autónoma de México, Mexico
Vanessa Gore, Australia

Peter Graefe, McMaster University, Canada
Rachael Gray, Australia
Laura Grenfell, University of Adelaide, Australia
José de Jesús Gudiño Pelayo, Suprema Corte de Justicia de la Nación, Mexico
Virgilio Guimarães, Governo do Brazil, Brazil
Jim Hancock, South Australian Centre for Economic Studies, Australia
Tom Henderson, National Center for State Courts, United States
Meenakshi Hooja, Government of Rajasthan, India
Rakesh Hooja, Government of India, India
Paul Huber, Regierungsrat des Kantons Luzern (former), Switzerland
Siraj Hussain, Hamdard University, India
Jordi Jané, Congreso de los Diputados, Spain
Priscilla Jebaraj, CNBC India, India
Nirmal Jindal, Delhi University, India
Nelson Jobim, Corte Suprema do Brazil, Brazil
Hayden Jones, Tasmanian State Government, Australia
Sindhu Joy, University of Kerala, India
Subhash C. Kashyap, Parliament of India (former), India ·
Ellis Katz, Temple University, United States
Markus Kern, Université de Fribourg, Switzerland
Arshi Khan, Hamdard University, India
John Kincaid, Lafayette College, United States
Jutta Kramer, Universität Hannover, Germany
Nicolas Lagasse, Facultés Universitaires Saint-Louis, Belgium
Harvey Lazar, Queen's University, Canada
J. Wesley Leckrone, Temple University, United States
Oryssia Lennie, Western Economic Diversification Canada, Canada
Geoff Lindell, University of Adelaide, Australia
Bruno Lombaert, Facultés Universitaires Saint-Louis, Belgium
Augustin Macheret, Université de Fribourg, Switzerland
Clem Macintyre, University of Adelaide, Australia
Akhtar Majeed, Hamdard University, India
Ignasi Manrubia, Spain
Jospeh Marbach, Seton Hall University, United States
George Mathew, Institute of Social Sciences, India
Stephen McDonald, University of Adelaide, Australia
Ully C. Merkel, Australia
Mônica Mora, Instituto de Pesquisa Econômica Aplicada, Brazil
Jacqueline Muniz, Governo do Brazil, Brazil
Francesc Muñoz, Spain
Alhaji Ghali Na'abba, National Assembly, Nigeria
Adam Nagler, Government of Ontario, Canada
A.S. Narang, Indira Gandhi National Open University, India

Amy Nugent, University of Toronto, Canada
Nurudeen A. Ogbara, National Association of Democratic Lawyers, Nigeria
Ajene Ogiri, Benue State Government, Nigeria
Georg-Berndt Oschatz, Bundesrat (former), Germany
Sam Oyovbaire, TAS Associates, Nigeria
Martin Papillon, University of Toronto, Canada
Arijit Pasayat, Supreme Court of India, India
Tom Pauling, Government of Northern Territory, Australia
Malte Pehl, Universität Heidelberg, Germany
Anna Peliano, Instituto de Pesquisa Econômica Aplicada, Brazil
Marcelo Piancastelli de Siqueira, Instituto de Pesquisa Econômica Aplicada, Brazil
Patricia Popelier, Universiteit Antwerpen, Belgium
Sérgio Prado, Universidade Estadual de Campinas, Brazil
Michael Prince, University of Victoria, Canada
Ranjita Rajan, India
C. Rangarajan, XIIth Finance Commission, India
A.K. Rastogi, Government of India, India
David Renders, Université Catholique de Louvain, Belgium
Fernando Rezende, Fundação Getulio Vargas, Brazil
Christian E. Rieck, Humboldt-Universität zu Berlin, Germany
Horst Risse, Bundesrat, Germany
Marcial Rodríguez Saldaña, Ayuntamiento de Acapulco, Mexico
Eduard Roig, Universitat de Barcelona, Spain
Géraldine Rosoux, Université de Liège, Belgium
Ash Narain Roy, Institute of Social Sciences, India
Cheryl Saunders, University of Melbourne, Australia
Rekha Saxena, University of Delhi, India
Annemie Schauss, Université Libre de Bruxelles, Belgium
Stephen L. Schechter, Russell Sage College, United States
Hans-Peter Schneider, Universität Hannover, Germany
Jean-Claude Scholsem, Université de Liège, Belgium
Brad Selway, Federal Court of Australia, Australia
Sandeep Shastri, International Academy for Creative Teaching, India
Kenneth Shear, Philadelphia Bar Association, United States
Richard E.B. Simeon, University of Toronto, Canada
Julie Simmons, Guelph University, Canada
M.P. Singh, Delhi University, India
Ajay K. Singh, Hamdard University, India
Santosh Singh, Institute of Social Sciences, India
Jennifer Smith, Dalhousie University, Canada
Troy E. Smith, Drury University, United States
Saifuddin Soz, Parliament of India, India

Nico Steytler, University of the Western Cape, South Africa
Kumar Suresh, Hamdard University, India
Johan Swinnen, Gouvernement fédéral, Belgium
Bruce Tait, Government of Alberta, Canada
G. Alan Tarr, Rutgers University, United States
Victor Tootoo, Government of Nunavut, Canada
Joaquim Tornos, Generalitat de Catalunya, Spain
Dircêo Torrecillas Ramos, Fundação Getulio Vargas, Brazil
Paola Torres Robles, Instituto para el Desarrollo Técnico de las Haciendas
Públicas, Mexico
François Tulkens, Facultés Universitaires Saint-Louis, Belgium
Judy Tyers, Government of Victoria (former), Australia
Bala Usman, Ahmadu Bello University, Nigeria
Clemente Valdez Sánchez, Mexico
Marc Van der Hulst, Belgische Kamer van Volksvertegenwoordigers, Belgium
Sébastien Van Drooghenbroeck, Facultés Universitaires Saint-Louis, Belgium
Damien van Eyll, Gouvernement fédéral, Belgium
Jeroen Van Nieuwenhove, Raad van State, Belgium
Patrick van Ypersele, Chambre des Représentants, Belgium
Manu Vandenbossche, Universiteit Brussel, Belgium
Ricardo Varsano, Instituto de Pesquisa Econômica Aplicada, Brazil
Clara Velasco Rico, Universitat Pompeu Fabra, Spain
M.N. Venkatachaliah, National Commission to Review the Working of the
Constitution, India
Michael Vethasiromony, Government of Kerala, India
Joan Vintró, Parlament de Catalunya, Spain
Carles Viver, Institut d'Estudis Autonòmics, Spain
Donatienne Wahl, Conseil de la Région Bruxelles-Capitale, Belgium
Ronald Watts, Queen's University, Canada
Conrad Weiler, Temple University, United States
Paul Weizer, Fitchburg State College, United States
Fiona Wheeler, Australian National University, Australia
John White, Saskatchewan Institute of Public Policy, Canada
John Williams, University of Adelaide, Australia
Mark Winfield, Pembina Institute for Appropriate Development, Canada
Vicente Y Pla Trevas, Presidência da República, Brazil
Farah Abdullah Yasmin, India
Lars Zimmermann, Aspen Institute Berlin, Germany

Distribution of Powers and Responsibilities in Federal Countries
Edited by Akhtar Majeed, Ronald L. Watts, and Douglas M. Brown
Senior Editor, John Kincaid

Published for the Forum of Federations and the International Association of Centers for Federal Studies (IACFS)
A Global Dialogue on Federalism, Book Series, Volume 2

The comparative studies in this volume examine the distribution of exclusive and shared powers and responsibilities among the national and constituent governments in 11 diverse federal countries: Australia, Belgium, Brazil, Canada, Germany, India, Mexico, Nigeria, Spain, Switzerland, and the United States. Each chapter examines the constitutional distribution of powers, reasons for the distribution, changes in the distribution of powers over time, and actual workings of the distribution of powers. The chapters also address the success or failure of each country's system of power distribution and point toward likely future trends in the allocation and sharing of powers in each country.

DOUGLAS M. BROWN is fellow, Institute of Intergovernmental Relations and Adjunct Associate Professor, School of Policy Studies, Queen's University, Kingston, Canada.
AKHTAR MAJEED is professor of Political Science and Director of the Centre for Federal Studies at Hamdard University in New Delhi, India.
RONALD L. WATTS is principal emeritus and professor emeritus of political studies, Queen's University, Kingston, Canada.

October 2005
0-7735-2974-8
6 x 9 11 maps

The French edition of this book, *Partage des compétences dans les pays fédéraux,* will be available in 2006.

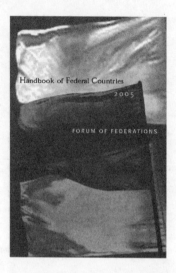

Handbook of Federal Countries, 2005
Edited by Ann L. Griffiths, Coordinated by Karl Nerenberg

An indispensable reference book on the developments, political dynamics,
institutions, and constitutions of the world's federal countries.

Published for the Forum of Federations

For more than two centuries federalism has provided an example of how people can live
together even as they maintain their diversity. *The Handbook of Federal Countries, 2005*
continues the tradition started by the 2002 edition, updating and building on the work
of Ronald Watts and Daniel Elazar in providing a comparative examination of countries
organized on the federal principle.

Unique in its timely scope and depth, this volume includes a foreword by Forum
President Bob Rae that reflects on the importance of the federal idea in the
contemporary world. New comparative chapters examine the recent draft constitutional
treaty in Europe and the possibility of federalism being adopted in two countries with
longstanding violent conflicts – Sri Lanka and Sudan.

As a project of the Forum of Federations, an international network on federalism in
practice, the 2005 handbook is an essential sourcebook of information, with maps and
statistical tables in each chapter.

ANN GRIFFITHS is professor, Dalhousie College of Continuing Education, Dalhousie
University.
KARL NERENBERG is director of public information and senior editor, Forum of
Federations.

0-7735-2888-1
6 x 9 488pp 30 maps
French edition: *Guide des pays fédéraux, 2005*
0-7735-2896-2